Time-Si for Teachers

SPELLING YEARS 1-2

Peter Clutterbuck

W
FRANKLIN WATTS
LONDON • SYDNEY

How to use this book

This book provides a range of worksheets suitable for children in Years 1 and 2 of primary school. The worksheets are grouped into sections that correspond to the word level work specified in the National Literacy Strategy. The contents are equally relevant to the Scottish 5–14 Guidelines, and the curricula for the Republic and Northern Ireland.

Each section starts with an *introduction* that sets the topic in context. The worksheets that follow are mostly laid out in pairs, with the left- and right-hand pages catering for *different* levels of ability. Complete *answers* are provided to save time with marking. You can then keep the worksheets as part of the pupils' *assessment* records.

All teacher pages have a vertical stripe down the side of the page. All the worksheets are photocopiable.

This edition first published in 2004

Franklin Watts
96 Leonard Street, London EC2A 4XD

UK adaptation by Brenda Stones
Educational advisers: Sarah St John, Jo Owston

This edition not for sale outside the United Kingdom and Eire

ISBN 0 7496 5801 0

Printed in Dubai

Contents

High frequency words for word recognition from Reception year

National Literacy Strategy Framework

Reception year

I	go	come	went	up	you	day	was
look	are	the	of	we	this	dog	me
like	going	big	she	and	they	my	see
on	away	mum	it	at	play	no	yes
for	a	dad	can	he	am	all	
is	cat	get	said	to	in		

High frequency words for word recognition Years 1-2

National Literacy Strategy Framework

Years 1-2

about	can't	her	many	over	then	who
after	could	here	may	people	there	will
again	did	him	more	push	these	with
an	do	his	much	pull	three	would
another	don't	home	must	put	time	your
as	dig	house	name	ran	too	
back	door	how	new	saw	took	
ball	down	if	next	school	tree	
be	first	jump	night	seen	two	
because	from	just	not	should	us	
bed	girl	last	now	sister	very	
been	good	laugh	off	so	want	
boy	got	little	old	some	water	
brother	had	live(d)	once	take	way	
but	half	love	one	than	were	
by	has	made	or	that	what	
call(ed)	have	make	our	their	when	
came	help	man	out	them	where	

Summary of the specific phonics and spelling work to be covered in Years 1–2

Year 1

Term 1

Practise and reinforce work from YR

Discriminate, write and read middle (short vowel) sounds in simple words:

'a' (fat), 'e' (wet), 'i' (pig),

'o' (pot), 'u' (mug)

Term 2

Practise and reinforce work from Y1 Term 1

Read and spell words ending in ck, ff, ll, ss, ng

Discriminate, blend and spell initial consonant clusters:

bl, br, cl, cr, dr, dw, fl, fr, gl, gr, pl, pr, sc, scr, sk, sl, sm, sn, sp,

spl, spr, squ, st, str, sw, tr, tw, thr, shr, and common end clusters: ld,

nd, lk, nk, sk, lp, mp, sp, ct, ft, lt, nt, pt, st, xt, lf, nch, lth

Term 3

Practise and reinforce work from Y1 Term 2

Discriminate, spell and read the common spelling patterns for the long vowel

phonemes: 'ee', 'ai', 'ie', 'oa', 'oo':

ee: 'ee' (feet), 'ea' (seat)

ai: 'ai' (train), 'a-e' (name), 'ay' (play)

ie: 'ie' (lie), 'i-e' (bite), 'igh' (high), 'y' (fly)

oa: 'oa' (boat), 'o-e' (pole), 'ow' (show)

oo: 'oo' (moon), 'u-e' (tune), 'ew' (flew), 'ue' (blue)

Year 2

Term 1

Practise and reinforce long vowel work from Y1 Term 3 above

Discriminate, spell and read the common spelling patterns for the vowel

phonemes: 'oo' (short), 'ar', 'oy', 'ow':

oo (short): 'u' (pull), 'oo' (good)

ar: 'ar' (car)

oy: 'oi' (boil), 'oy' (toy)

ow: 'ow' (cow), 'ou' (sound)

Term 2

Practise and reinforce work from Y2 Term 1

Discriminate, spell and read the common spelling patterns for the vowel

phonemes: 'air', 'or', 'er'

air: 'air' (fair), 'are' (scare), 'ere' (there), 'ear' (bear, wear)

or: 'or' (sport), 'oor' (floor), 'aw' (claw), 'au' (caught), 'ore' (more, store)

er: 'er' (her, were), 'ir' (bird), 'ur' (fur)

Term 3

Practise and reinforce work from previous terms

Discriminate, spell and read the common spelling patterns for the vowel

phonemes: 'ear', 'ea'

ear: e.g. fear, hear

ea: (bread, head)

Introduction and Answers to Alphabetic Knowledge

National Literacy Strategy objectives

In Reception year, the National Literacy Strategy expected teachers to have introduced the alphabet as follows:

YR W3: alphabetic and phonic knowledge through:

sounding and naming each letter of the alphabet in lower and upper case;

writing letters in response to letter names;

understanding alphabetical order through alphabet books, rhymes, and songs.

At the beginning of Year 1, you would expect to take this forward:

Y1T1 W2: from YR, to practise and secure alphabetic letter knowledge and alphabetic order.

The distinction between vowels and consonants is formally introduced at the end of Year 1:

Y1T3 W9: the terms 'vowel' and 'consonant'.

Introducing the alphabet

There is a whole range of techniques to help reinforce pupils' knowledge of how letters convey sounds (the 'grapheme/phoneme correspondence'):

● wall friezes ● alphabet books ● using pupils' names for initial letter sounds

The worksheets

The sheets in this section practise 14 consonants.

Answers to page 9

girl, goat; fan, feather, fox

Answers to page 10

books, ball, box; car, cup, cat

Answers to page 11

mask, man, mouse; letter, leg, lamp

Answers to page 12

pig, peg, pear; ring, rain, rabbit

Answers to page 13

snake, starfish, sun; hat, house, hand

Answers to page 14

two, tree, tap; watch, whistle, wand

Answers to page 15

drum, doll, duck; nest, net, nut

Alphabetic Knowledge

Name _____

Circle the pictures that begin with **g**.

g

 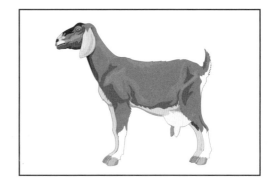

 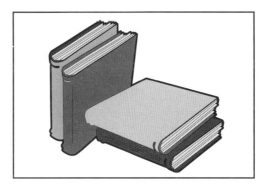

Circle the pictures that begin with ƒ.

ƒ

 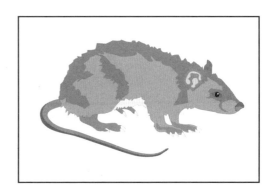

Alphabetic Knowledge

Name _____

Circle the pictures that begin with **b**.

b

 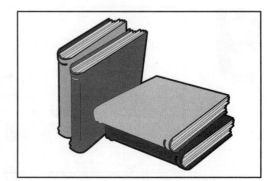

 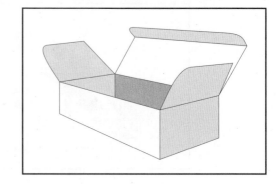

Circle the pictures that begin with **c**.

c

 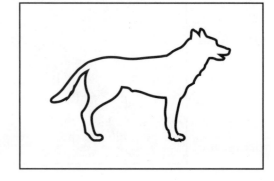

Alphabetic Knowledge

Name _____

Circle the pictures that begin with **m**.

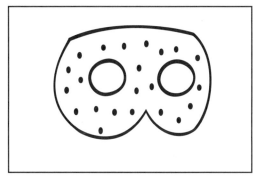
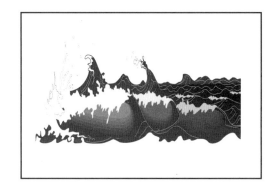

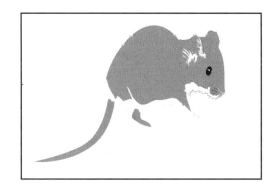

Circle the pictures that begin with **l**.

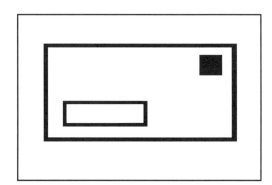

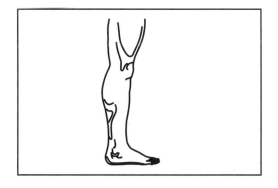
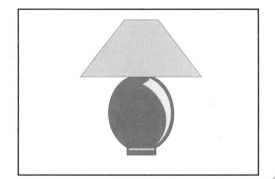

Alphabetic Knowledge

Name _____

Circle the pictures that begin with **p**.

p

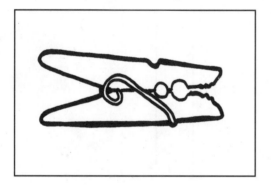

Circle the pictures that begin with r.

r

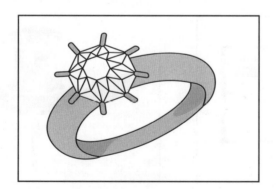

Alphabetic Knowledge

Name _____

Circle the pictures that begin with **s**.

s

Circle the pictures that begin with **h**.

h

 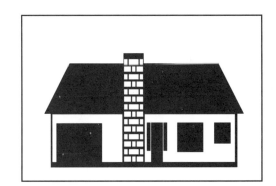

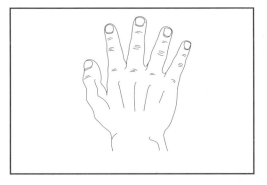 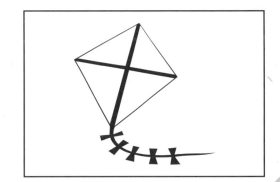

13

Alphabetic Knowledge

Name _____

Circle the pictures that begin with **t**.

Circle the pictures that begin with **w**.

 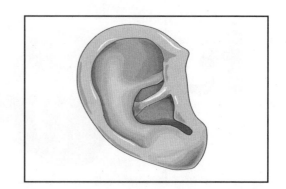

 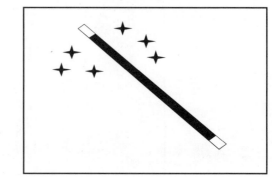

Alphabetic Knowledge

Name _____

Circle the pictures that begin with **d**.

d

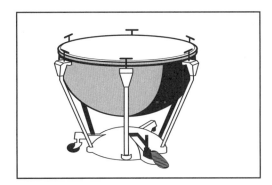 

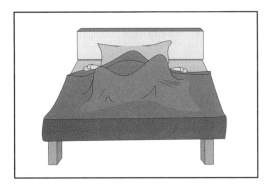 

Circle the pictures that begin with **n**.

n

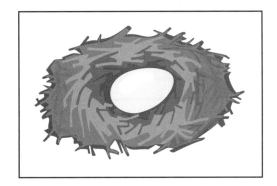 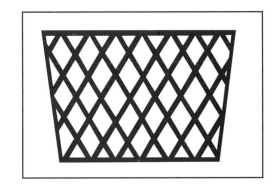

 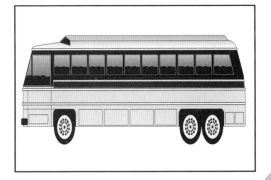

Introduction to CVC Words

National Literacy Strategy objectives

Although the National Literacy Strategy expects the CVC pattern (Consonant Vowel Consonant) to have been introduced in Reception year, most work on CVC words will be done in Year 1 Term 1:

Y1T1 W3: from YR, to practise and secure the ability to hear initial and final phonemes in CVC words, e.g. fit, mat, pan;

Y1T1 W4: to discriminate and segment all three phonemes in CVC words;

Y1T1 W5: to blend phonemes to read CVC words in rhyming and non-rhyming sets.

Introducing CVC words

The most common approach to helping children to read and write CVC words is to build a collection of families of rhyming words, e.g. bat, cat, hat, before learning to distinguish the initial consonants.

This way of breaking the words is called 'onset and rime', the 'rime' being the end vowel and consonant, and the 'onset' the initial consonant.

The worksheets

The worksheets progress in difficulty through the section.

Pages 17–18 offer practice in copying simple CVC words, using picture cues.

Page 26 is the key page for practising onset and rime.

The other pages mix practice in medial vowels and the other individual phonemes in CVC words.

CVC Words

Name _____

Look at the words in each box. Write the correct word beside each picture.

1.

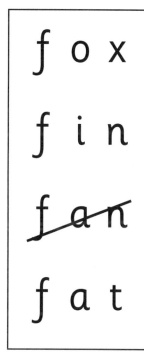

| |
| f o x |
| f i n |
| ~~f a n~~ |
| f a t |

a. _f a n_

b. _____

c. _____

d. _____

2.

| |
| s u n |
| s a d |
| s i x |
| s i t |

a. _____

b. _____

c. _____

d. _____

CVC Words

Name _____

Look at the words in each box. Write the correct word beside each picture.

1.

p a n
~~p e n~~
p i n
p i g

a.  _____

b. _____

c. _____

d. _____

2.

b e d
b o x
b u g
b a g

a. _____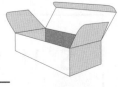

b. _____

c. _____

d. _____

CVC Words

Name _____

1. Circle the word that does not begin with the same letter.

   a. map   men   mix   (top)

   b. wet   ten   wig   win

   c. bed   box   cup   bun

   d. ram   rod   pig   red

   e. pin   log   pet   pot

   f. tip   ten   tag   rug

2. Complete each word.

   a. pi_**g**_    d. tu_____

   b. ro_____    e. li_____

   c. pi_____   f. ca_____

CVC Words

Name _____

1. Choose the correct letter to complete each word.

a. (d   b)

___ed

b. (b   l)

___eg

c. (h   c)

___ut

d. (m   h)

___en

2. Find 4 words in the box. Write each beside its picture.

pencatbusfan

a.

_____

b.

_____

c.

_____

d.

_____

CVC Words

Name _____

1. Join the letters to make words.

a.
t — ap **tap**
t — en _____
t — ug _____

b.
p — en _____
p — ig _____
p — up _____

c.
b — ox _____
b — un _____
b — us _____

d.
h — en _____
h — ot _____
h — ug _____

2. Add a letter to finish each word.

a. __**t**__ en

b. _____ en

c. _____ in

d. _____ ut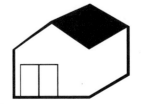

21

CVC Words

Name _____

1. Make words to match the pictures. Use one letter from each box.

c	u	t
b	a	x
s	o	n

a. **sun**

b. _____

c. _____

2. Circle the word that matches the picture.

nip   net   (nut)

a. leg lip log

b. leg lip log

c. leg

lip

log

d. nip   net   nut

CVC Words

Name _____

1. **Circle the word that matches the picture.**

a. (bed) bad big b. peg pig pup

c. ten top tap d. cot cow cup

e. den dog dot f. red ram rod

2. **Complete each word.**

a. p _i_ g  b. m ___ p

c. t ___ p   d. j ___ t

23

CVC Words

Name _____

1. **Complete each sentence.**

   Use these words.

   | fox   mop   peg   rug   ~~fan~~ |

   This is a **fan** .

   a. This is a _____ .   b. This is a _____ .

   c. This is a _____ .   d. This is a _____ .

2. **Unjumble these letters to make words.**

   a. lge    b. xsi

   ___**leg**___   _____

   c. bga    d. htu

   _____   _____

CVC Words

Name _____

1. Join the words that rhyme.

a.
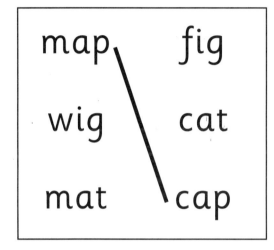

map   fig

wig   cat

mat   cap

b.

sun   hen

den   cut

nut   fun

2. Find words that match the pictures. Write the words in the spaces.

l	i	p	h
c	b	p	e
a	e	a	n
t	d	n	x

 _____

 _____

 _____

 _____

 _____

25

CVC Words

Name _____

Change the first letter of each word to make a new one.
Use the picture clues to help you.

a. leg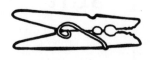

    _p_ eg

b. hat

    ___at

c. box

    ___ox

d. but

    ___ut

e. got

    ___ot

f. red

    ___ed

CVC Words

Name _____

Change the middle letter of each word to make a new one.
Use the picture clues to help you.

a. fit

f <u>**a**</u> t

b. but

b ___ t

c. cap

c ___ p

d. hit

h ___ t

e. bad

b ___ d

f. top

t ___ p

g. son

s ___ n

h. tan

t ___ n

CVC Words

Name _____

Change the last letter of each word to make a new one.
Use the picture clues to help you.

a. can

ca **p**

b. let

le___

c. run

ru___

d. pin

pi___

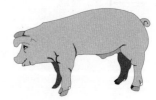

e. hem

he___

f. fog

fo___

CVC Words

Name _____

Look at each picture and sound out its first letter. Write each first letter in the box to make a new word. The first one has been done for you.

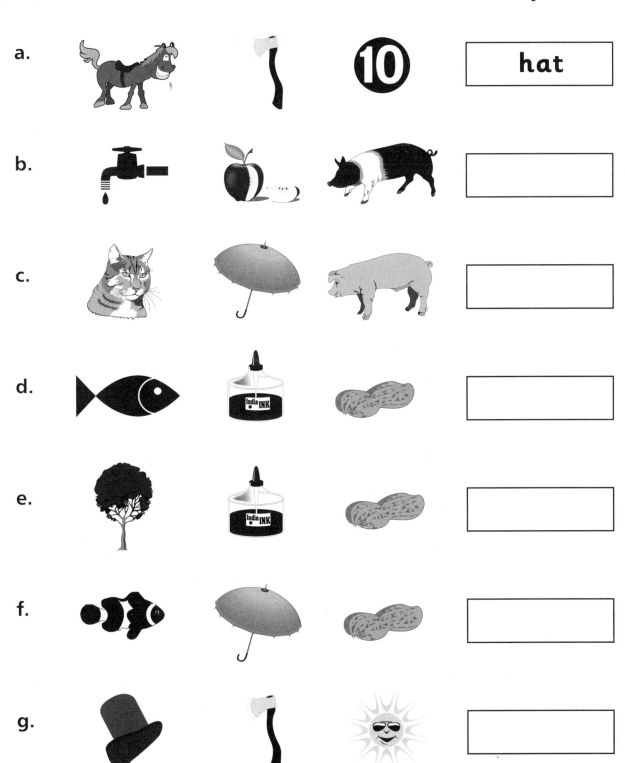

a.   hat

CVC Words

Name _____

Unjumble the letters to make a word that matches the picture.
The first one has been done for you.

a. tnu

_____

b. tca

_____

c. dgo

_____

d. tpa

_____

e. fxo

_____

f. tha

_____

g. glo

_____

h. lge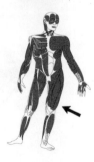

_____

i. nte

_____

j. uns

_____

Answers to CVC Words

Answers to page 17

1 fat, fin, fox

2 sad, sun, sit, six

Answers to page 18

1 pan, pig, pin

2 box, bug, bed, bag

Answers to page 19

1 ten, cup, pig, log, rug

2 rod, pin, tug, lip, cat

Answers to page 20

1 bed, leg, hut, hen

2 fan, bus, cat, pen

Answers to page 21

1 ten, tug; pen, pig, pup; box, bun, bus; hen, hot, hug

2 men, fin, hut

Answers to page 22

1 box, cat

2 lip, log, leg, net

Answers to page 23

1 peg, tap, cup, dog, rod

2 map, top, jet

Answers to page 24

1 peg, rug, fox, mop

2 six, bag, hut

Answers to page 25

1 wig, fig; mat, cat; sun, fun; den, hen; nut, cut

2 cat, bed, pan, lip, hen

Answers to page 26

cat, fox, cut, cot, bed

Answers to page 27

bat, cup, hot, bed, tap, sun, ten

Answers to page 28

leg, rug, pig, hen, fox

Answers to page 29

tap, cup, fin, tin, fun, has

Answers to page 30

nut, cat, dog, tap, fox, hat, log, leg, ten, sun

Introduction to Consonant Clusters

National Literacy Strategy objectives

The National Literacy Strategy distinguishes between word endings with combined consonants but a single sound:

Y1T2 W2: to investigate, read and spell words ending in ff, ll, ss, ck, ng;

and those with more than one sound or phoneme, properly called consonant clusters:

Y1T2 W3: to discriminate, read and spell words with initial consonant clusters, e.g. bl, cr, tr, str;

to discriminate, read and spell words with final consonant clusters, e.g. nd, lp, st.

The full list of initial and end consonant clusters from 'List 3' can be found on page 6.

Introducing consonant clusters

You could start by inviting the class to brainstorm all the words they can think of beginning with each of the initial consonant clusters; and then all those they know of with the listed end clusters. These lists could be displayed and added to throughout the year.

The worksheets

This section covers intensively all the consonant clusters listed for Year 1 Term 2 in the National Literacy Strategy Framework (see page 6 of this book). The clusters are used at both the beginning and ends of words.

Consonant Clusters

Name _____

1. **Complete each word.**

   Use these letters.

br	cr	fr	pl	st	~~sn~~

   a. **s** **n** ake

   b. ___ ___ og

   c. ___ ___ ab

   d. ___ ___ ay

   e. ___ ___ oom

   f. ___ ___ ar

2. **Complete each word.**

   Use these letters.

~~ll~~	ck	ll	nt	th	ch

   a. be**ll**

   b. bu___ ___

   c. du___ ___

   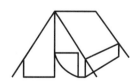
   d. te___ ___

   e. mo___ ___

   f. ___ ___ in

Consonant Clusters

Name _____

1. **Choose the correct ending to complete each word. Write it in the space.**

   a. (st nd)

   ne **st**

   b. (ft mp)

   la____

   c. (ng sh)

   wi____

   d. (ch sh)

   fi____

2. **Unjumble the letters to make words to match the pictures.**

   a. (cklo)

   lock

   b. (ipsh)

   _____

   c. (lldo)

   _____

   d. (thmo)

   _____

Consonant Clusters

Name _____

1. **Circle the word that matches the picture.**

a. wing
(swing)
sing
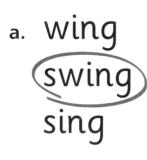

b. sock
rock
lock

c. shed
ship
stop
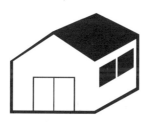

d. bath
path
moth

e. pull
bull
full

f. duck
luck
sick

2. **Circle the word that does not have the same ending.**

e.g.   best   must   (crab)   lost

a. soft   sift   nest   lift
b. wish   dish   wash   bill
c. limp   band   hand   land
d. cloth   wing   sing   string

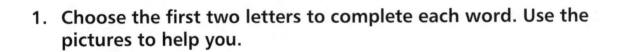

Consonant Clusters

Name _____

1. **Choose the first two letters to complete each word. Use the pictures to help you.**

   a. (bl cr)

   _____y

   b. (dr cr)

   _____ip

   c. (fl cl)

   _____ag

   d. (sk st)

   _____ool

2. **Make three words that start with the same letters.**

   Use these letters.

sk	fr	st	tr

   a. **sk** in   b. _____og   c. _____ep   d. _____ee

   sk y   _____ock   _____ar   _____y

   sk ip   _____ee   _____op   _____ip

3. **Look at the pictures. Complete each word.**

   a. _____oom   b. _____ow

Consonant Clusters

Name _____

1. **Match each word to its meaning.**

| frock story sty spin |

   a. to turn quickly _____   **c.** a tale _____

   b. pigs' home _____   **d.** a dress _____

2. **Complete each word using the letters in the box.**

| st sk tr cr sp cr |

a. ___ ___ip

b. ___ ___ay

c. ___ ___reet

d. ___ ___ash

e. ___ ___y

f. ___ ___ace

3. **Add Box A to Box B to make words, then write each word on a line.**

Box A	Box B
sp	eed
cl	ay
dr	ag
gr	ab

   _____

   _____

   _____

   _____

Consonant Clusters

Name _____

1. **Write each word next to its meaning.**

| blue   stream   fly   straw   pram   plum |

   a. a baby carriage _____
        d. a small river _____

   b. dry grass _____
              e. a colour _____

   c. an insect _____
           f. a fruit _____

2. **Complete each word.**

   a. (cr pl)

        b. (br fl)

   _____ant
                  _____ick

   c. (pl pr)

        d. (dr br)

   _____ay
                  _____um

3. **Write in pairs the words that begin with the same letters.**

| drag   place   stuck   broom |
| steep   broke   plan   drop |

_____   _____

_____   _____

Consonant Clusters

Name _____

1. **Find words in the grid. Write each beside the correct picture.**

c	l	o	c	k
d	r	u	m	s
f	l	a	g	t
f	r	o	g	a
c	r	o	w	r

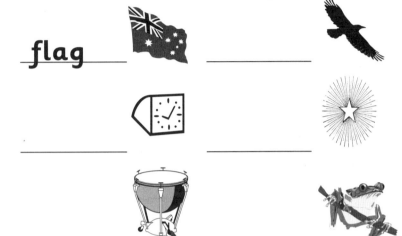

flag _____   _____

_____   _____

_____   _____

2. **Complete each word.**

Use these letters.

tr   pl   dr   fl

a. ___ ___ agon    b. ___ ___ ane

c. ___ ___ y   d. ___ ___ ee

3. **Write each word beside the correct picture.**

crab   broom   block   pram

a. _____   b. _____

c. _____   d. _____

Consonant Clusters

Name _____

1. Find all the words in the grid that end in **st**. Write them in the spaces.

n	e	s	t	a	j	m
l	p	r	l	r	u	o
o	e	e	i	u	s	s
s	s	s	s	s	t	t
t	t	t	t	t	x	x

nest _____   _____

_____   _____

_____   _____

_____   _____

2. Colour in blue the words that end in **nt**. Colour in red the words that end in **nk**.

bank	bent	went
hunt	ink	sink
drink	wink	plant
ant	pink	blunt

3. Write in pairs the words that end in the same way.

stamp gift desk bolt
lift melt mask bump

_____   _____   _____   _____

_____   _____   _____   _____

Consonant Clusters

Name _____

1. Write each word under the correct picture.

| pond   mask   plant |

a. _____   b. _____   c. _____

2. Complete each sentence.

| gift   soft   colt   left |

a. I have a right hand and a _____ hand.

b. A _____ is a young horse.

c. My grandma gave me a _____ for Christmas.

d. This metal is hard but this wool is _____.

3. Write each word under the correct picture.

| stamp   desk   lamp |

a. _____   b. _____   c. _____

Consonant Clusters

Name _____

Complete each word. Use the picture clues to help you.

1.

Use these letters.

wh	ck	thr	gr

a. du_____

b. _____one

c. _____ub

d. _____istle

2.

tr	sw	sk	cl

a. _____an

b. _____ull

c. _____ock

d. _____actor

3.

dr	st	dr	tw

a. _____ar

b. _____agon

c. _____enty   20

d. _____um

Consonant Clusters

Name _____

Write the first two letters of the first word. Then write the first letter of the next two words. Write all four letters to make a new word.

| c | l | + | a | + | p | = | clap |

a. ☐☐ + ☐ + ☐ = ☐

b. ☐☐ + ☐ + ☐ = ☐

c. ☐☐ + ☐ + ☐ = ☐

d. ☐☐ + ☐ + ☐ = ☐

e. ☐☐ + ☐ + ☐ = ☐

Consonant Clusters

Name _____

Add the pieces to make a word. Write the word and draw the picture.

c + ake

= **cake**

a. tr + ain

=

b. fl + y

=

c. ch + icken

=

d. sh + ell

=

e. gl + ove

=

f. tw + elve

=

g. dr + ess

=

h. pr + am

=

Answers to Consonant Clusters

Answers to page 33

1 frog, crab, play, broom, star

2 bull, duck, tent, moth, chin

Answers to page 34

1 lamp, wing, fish

2 ship, doll, moth

Answers to page 35

1 sock, shed, bath, full, duck

2 nest, bill, limp, cloth

Answers to page 36

1 cry, drip, flag, stool

2 frog, frock, free; step, star, stop; tree, try, trip

3 broom, crow

Answers to page 37

1 spin, sty, story, frock

2 skip, tray, street, crash, cry, space

3 speed, clay, drag, grab

Answers to page 38

1 pram, straw, fly, stream, blue, plum

2 plant, brick, pray, drum

3 drag, drop; place, plan; stuck, street; broom, broke

Answers to page 39

1 clock, drum, crow, star, frog

2 dragon, plane, fly, tree

3 block, crab, pram, broom

Answers to page 40

1 nest, lost, pest, rest, list, rust, just, most

2 blue: bent, went, hunt, plant, ant, blunt

red: bank, ink, sink, drink, wink, pink

3 stamp, bump; gift, lift; desk, mask; bolt, melt

Answers to page 41

1 plant, pond, mask

2 left, colt, gift, soft

3 lamp, stamp, desk

Answers to page 42

1 duck, throne, grub, whistle

2 swan, skull, clock, tractor

3 star, dragon, twenty, drum

Answers to page 43

stop, skin, flat, drew, crab

Answers to page 44

train, fly, chicken, shell, glove, twelve, dress, pram

Introduction to Vowel Phonemes

National Literacy Strategy objectives

Most of the phonological awareness work for Year 2 is concentrated on vowel phonemes: both the different spellings for the same sound (oi and oy, ow and ou etc.) and the different sounds for the same spelling (e.g. ear and ea). The complete list of vowel phonemes in List 3 is reproduced on pages 6–7.

Introducing vowel phonemes

The sequence recommended is first the double vowels in Year 1 Term 3: ee, long oo, and then ai, oa and ie. In Year 2 Term 1 you can progress to short oo, ar, oy, ow; in Year 2 Term 2 to air, or, er; and in Year 2 Term 3 the tricky ear and ea.

Interestingly, there is no explicit reference in the National Literacy Strategy to 'magic e', i.e. the spelling rule for the long vowel phonemes a-e, i-e, o-e, u-e; but this rule is fundamental to many later rules involving short and long vowels, like gabble and gable, or mated and matted, and so it is recommended that 'magic e' is taught alongside the other long vowel phoneme sounds in Year 2.

The worksheets

The sheets in this section introduce most of the long and short vowel phonemes: ee, oo, ow, er, ar, and then pairings of a-e and ai, o-e and oa, and i-e.

Vowel Phonemes

Name _____

1. **Write each word under the correct picture.**

   ee – words with a long **e** sound

queen	teeth	bee	sheep	wheel
feet	seed		cheese	three

   a. _____   b. _____   c. _____

   d. _____   e. _____   f. _____

   g. _____   h. _____   i. _____

2. **Tick each pair of words where the vowels sound the same. Put a cross if they don't sound the same.**

   a. boot   root   ☐   e. cool   book   ☐

   b. sharp   letter ☐   f. door   floor   ☐

   c. some   done   ☐   g. bee   knee   ☐

   d. track   truck   ☐   h. neck   peck   ☐

Vowel Phonemes

Name _____

1. Write **oo** or **ee** to complete each word.

a. sh____p   b. b_____

c. b____t   d. sp_____n

2. Write each word in its pattern. The first one has been done for you.

    ar words

    | card   yard   garden   park |

    a. y a r d   b.

    c.   d.

3. Circle the word that matches the picture.

    a. moon    b. queen

        spoon   green

    c. bark    d. shake

        dark   shark

Vowel Phonemes

Name _____

1. **Complete each sentence.**

   Use these words ending in **ow**.

throw	row	snow	grow
yellow	low	slow	show

   a. A tiger has black and _____ stripes.

   b. During winter _____ sometimes falls.

   c. I brought my new bike to school to _____ my classmates.

   d. I tried to _____ the ball over the roof.

   e. If you plant a seed it might _____.

   f. This shelf is high but the other one is _____.

   g. A mouse is quick but a snail is _____.

   h. We formed a straight _____ outside the canteen.

2. **These words all end in er. Write each beside its meaning.**

winter	river	summer	dinner	flower	tower

   a. a tall building _____

   b. a rose is one _____

   c. a hot season _____

   d. a cold season _____

   e. a meal of the day _____

   f. we can catch fish in it _____

From Time-Savers for Teachers: Spelling Years 1-2. This page may be reproduced for classroom use.

49

Vowel Phonemes

Name _____

1. Complete each word.

Use these letters.

ee   ai   oo   ea   ee   ar

a. sn_____l   b. s_____l   c. wh_____l

d. c_____p   e. s_____d   f. b_____k

2. Complete the word families.

Add these words.

sting   beat   flew   toil

a. seat   b. stew   c. sing   d. spoil
   meat   drew   thing   soil
   heat   few   wing   oil

_____   _____   _____   _____

3. Complete each word pair.

chew   coin   glove   boy

a. join   **coin**   c. few   _____

b. love   _____   d. joy   _____

Vowel Phonemes

Name _____

1. Write each word under the correct picture.

a followed by an **e** makes a long **a** sound

| plate   face   spade |

a. _____   b. _____   c. _____

2. Write each word under the correct picture.

oa – long **o** sound

| road   loaf   boat |

a. _____   b. _____   c. _____

3. Complete each sentence.

o + e – long **o** sound

| rose   bone   rode   smoke |

a. The _____ was coming from the fire.

b. A _____ is a beautiful flower.

c. The dog chewed the _____.

d. The girl _____ the horse.

Vowel Phonemes

Name _____

1. **Write each word under the correct picture.**

   i followed by an **e** makes a long **i** sound

   | kite   ice   bike   mice   nine   bite |

   a. _____   b. _____   c. _____

   d. _____   e. _____   f. _____

2. **Write each word under the correct picture.**

   ai words

   | nail   rain   train   snail   pain   tail |

   a. _____   b. _____   c. _____

   d. _____   e. _____   f. _____

Vowel Phonemes

Name _____

1. Circle the correct word.

   a. I dug the deep hole with a (**page** **spade**).

   b. During winter it may (**slow** **snow**).

   c. I (**found** **round**) a ten-pound note in the street.

   d. Susie sat on the (**neat** **seat**).

   e. I got two letters in the (**post** **ghost**).

2. Circle the two words that sound the same.

a. joy	dog	boy	**e.**	floor	sheep	door
b. raw	saw	cat	**f.**	hope	come	some
c. spoon	some	moon	**g.**	soon	moon	feet
d. tie	keep	deep	**h.**	nail	pail	coat

3. Complete each word.

Use these letters.

ai   ou   oa   ow

a. t_____l

b. r_____d

c. sn_____

d. cl_____d

Answers to Vowel Phonemes

Answers to page 47

1 bee, sheep, cheese, queen, teeth, three, feet, seed, wheel

2
Tick a, c, f, g, h
Cross b, d, e

Answers to page 48

1 sheep, bee, boot, spoon

2 yard, garden, card, park

3 moon, queen, bark, shark

Answers to page 49

1 yellow, snow, show, throw, grow, low, slow, row

2 tower, flower, summer, winter, dinner, river

Answers to page 50

1 snail, seal, wheel, carp, seed, book

2 beat, flew, sting, toil

3 glove, chew, boy

Answers to page 51

1 plate, spade, face

2 road, boat, loaf

3 smoke, rose, bone, rode

Answers to page 52

1 kite, bike, mice, ice, nine, bite

2 nail, rain, train, snail, tail, pain

Answers to page 53

1 spade, snow, found, seat, post

2
joy, boy;
raw, saw;
spoon, moon;
keep, deep;
floor, door;
come, some;
soon, moon;
nail, pail

3 tail, road, snow, cloud

Introduction to Identifying Phonemes

National Literacy Strategy objectives

At the end of Year 2, it is suggested that all the rules of phonemic spelling are revised:

Y2T3 W1: to secure phonemic spellings from previous 5 terms.

Introducing identifying phonemes

The previous three sections of the book studied CVC words, consonant clusters, and vowel phonemes. This section now helps children to separate, identify and distinguish the separate parts of the word: the 'onset' of the initial consonant or consonant cluster, the medial vowel, and the final consonant or consonant cluster.

The worksheets

The techniques used in this section include adding letters, making substitutions, rearranging letters and decoding picture cues. All these approaches should help reinforce the different patterns of letters in phonically regular words.

Identifying Phonemes

Name _____

Add a letter to make a new word that matches the picture.

a. all

___all

b. ate

___ate

c. and

___and

d. up

___up

e. ice

___ice

f. oat

___oat

g. ill

___ill

h. ox

___ox

i. at

___at

j. ear

___ear

Identifying Phonemes

Name _____

Change the first letter to make a new word.

a. pest

 n est

b. coat

 ___oat

c. tear

 ___ear

d. save

 ___ave

e. noon

 ___oon

f. nine

 ___ine

g. block

 ___lock

h. dream

 ___ream

i. bone

 ___one

j. better

 ___etter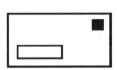

k. sing

 ___ing

l. mouse

 ___ouse

Identifying Phonemes

Name _____

Add a letter at the beginning of each word. Write the new word.

a. **s** eat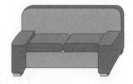

____**seat**____

b. ___one

_____

c. ___ice

_____

d. ___ear

_____

e. ___our

4

_____

f. ___rown

_____

g. ___read

_____

h. ___now

_____

i. ___oat

_____

j. ___ace

_____

k. ___owl

_____

l. ___our

_____

Identifying Phonemes

Name _____

Change the underlined letter to make a new word.

a. b<u>a</u>ll

b **e** ll

b. n<u>o</u>ne

n___ne

c. r<u>a</u>ng

r___ng

d. ma<u>r</u>k

ma___k

e. st<u>o</u>p

st___p

f. f<u>lo</u>g

fl___g

g. sh<u>o</u>p

sh___p

h. w<u>i</u>nd

w___nd

i. ha<u>r</u>d

ha___d

j. l<u>o</u>st

l___st

k. d<u>u</u>ll

d___ll

l. c<u>o</u>ke

c___ke

Identifying Phonemes

Name _____

Change the last letter to make a word that matches the picture.

a. cart

car **d**

b. root

roo___

c. wind

win___

d. hang

han___

e. book

boo___

f. feed

fee___

g. wool

woo___

h. tend

ten___

i. boar

boa___

j. bell

bel___

k. week

wee___

l. cool

coo___

Identifying Phonemes

Name _____

Add a letter to the end of each word. Write the new word.

a. car **d**

___**card**___

b. bat___

_____

c. stoo___

_____

d. ten___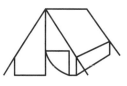

_____

e. win___

_____

f. can___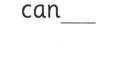

_____

g. see___

_____

h. far___

_____

i. bit___

_____

j. plan___

_____

k. pin___

_____

l. he___

_____

Identifying Phonemes

Name _____

Add a letter to each word. Make a new word to match the picture.

a. net

_____

b. fog

_____

c. fat

_____

d. seep

_____

e. hose

_____

f. sake

_____

g. wig

_____

h. hip

_____

i. cub

_____

j. sip

_____

k. pay

_____

l. sell

_____

Identifying Phonemes

Name _____

Make a new word using the first letter of each picture.
The first one has been done for you.

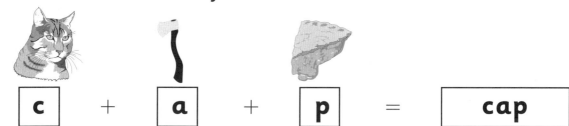

| c | + | a | + | p | = | cap |

a. ☐ + ☐ + ☐ + ☐ = ☐

b. ☐ + ☐ + ☐ + ☐ = ☐

c. ☐ + ☐ + ☐ + ☐ = ☐

d. ☐ + ☐ + ☐ + ☐ = ☐

e. ☐ + ☐ + ☐ + ☐ = ☐

Answers to Identifying Phonemes

Answers to page 56

ball, gate, hand, cup, mice, goat, hill, box, hat, bear

Answers to page 57

boat, bear, wave, moon, pine, clock, cream, cone, letter, ring, house

Answers to page 58

bone, mice, pear, four, crown, bread, snow, boat, race, bowl, pour

Answers to page 59

nine, ring, mask, step, flag, ship, wand, hand, list, doll, cake

Answers to page 60

roof, wing, hand, boot, feet, wood, tent, boat, belt, weep, cook

Answers to page 61

bath, stool, tent, wind, cane, seed, farm, bite, plant, pine, hen

Answers to page 62

nest, frog, fast, sheep, house, snake, wing, chip, club, ship, pray, shell

Answers to page 63

coat, ship, home, ring, name

Introduction and Answers to Double Consonants

National Literacy Strategy objectives

Double consonants are introduced quite early in Key Stage 1, alongside consonant clusters:

Y1T2 W2: to investigate, read and spell words ending in ff, ll, ss.

The worksheets

These pages start with double ll at the end of words, matching words ending with ff, ll and ss and more complex 'rimes'; and then anticipate double consonants in the middle of words.

Answers to page 66

1 wall, hill, well, doll

2 ball, fuss, off

Answers to page 67

1 bill, fill, pill, kill

2 moss, fuss;
otter, potter;
still, bill;
cross, grass;
mill, frill;
patter, clatter
rabbit, robber;

Answers to page 68

1 puppy, letter, bull, shell, hammer, button

2 summer, apple, kitten, lolly

3 sunny, shell, tall, little

Answers to page 69

1 jelly, middle, bell, butter, puppy, summer

2 kennel, summer, lolly, ball, hammer, tennis

3 jetty, glass, egg, happy, dinner, apple

Double Consonants

Name _____

1. Complete each word.

Use these endings.

ell   all   ill   oll

a. w_____

b. h_____

c. w_____

d. d_____

2. Look at the word at the top of each box.
Circle the word below it that is the same.

tell	**ball**	**fuss**	**off**
tin	been	first	old
(tell)	back	fuss	off
top	bone	from	out
tap	ball	four	one

From Time-Savers for Teachers: Spelling Years 1-2. This page may be reproduced for classroom use.

Double Consonants

Name _____

1. Complete each sentence.

Use these words.

| pill   bill   fill   kill |

a. A duck has a _____.

b. I am going to _____ the bottle with water.

c. The doctor gave the lady a _____.

d. The cat tried to _____ the bird.

2. Circle the words in each row that contain the same double consonants.

a. moss cart fuss dog

b. colt otter potter near

c. still may cave bill

d. cross send stew grass

e. mill bath frill cane

f. patter tooth clatter hair

g. rabbit cheese tail robber

Double Consonants

Name _____

1. **Write each word under its picture.**

| puppy   shell   letter   button   bull   hammer |

a. _____

b. _____

c. _____

d. _____

e. _____

f. _____

2. **Write each word beside its meaning.**

| apple   lolly   kitten   summer |

a. a hot season _____

c. baby cat _____

b. a fruit _____

d. a sweet _____

3. **Complete each sentence.**

| little   sunny   tall   shell |

a. It is warm and _____ today.

b. A snail carries its _____ on its back.

c. Tom is short but Ravi is _____.

d. An elephant is big but a mouse is _____.

Double Consonants

Name _____

1. **Circle the correct word in each sentence.**

   a. I ate some (jelly jolly) for tea.

   b. The centre of a circle is called the (middle muddle).

   c. We rang the (bell ball) at ten o'clock.

   d. I spread the (bitter butter) on the bread.

   e. A baby dog is called a (pippy puppy).

   f. It becomes very hot in (simmer summer).

2. **Add nn, ll or mm to make the word fit the meaning.**

   a. ke__ __el   a dog's home   d. ba__ __   it bounces

   b. su__ __er   a hot season   e. ha__ __er   a tool

   c. lo__ __y   a sweet food   f. te__ __is   a sport

3. **Complete each sentence using these words.**

happy jetty dinner glass apple egg

   a. The boat is tied up at the _____.

   b. If you drop a _____ it will break.

   c. My hen laid an _____.

   d. Tom is sad but Sally is _____.

   e. We are having fish for _____.

   f. An _____ is a type of fruit.

Introduction and Answers to Plurals with s

National Literacy Strategy objectives

The concept of simple plurals is also introduced early in Year 1:

Y1T2 W8: to investigate and learn spellings of words with s for plurals.

The worksheets

The first sheet uses numbers throughout to indicate plurals; the second sheet introduces the concepts of 'several' and 'many', and also suggests that children draw the multiple objects.

Answers to page 71

cats, flowers, hats,
cars, hens, dolls, cows,
trees, balls

Answers to page 72

books, stools,
hens, trees, papers,
flowers, cats

Plurals with s

Add an **s** to each word to make each word mean more than one.

a.

one **dog**   two **dogs** _____

b.

one **cat**   three _____

c.

one **flower**   four _____

d.

one **hat**   five _____

e.

one **car**   two _____

f.

one **hen**   four _____

g.

one **doll**   two _____

h.

one **cow**   two _____

i.

one **tree**   three _____

j.

one **ball**   five _____

71

Plurals with s

Make each word mean more than one. Draw the picture.
The first one has been done for you.

a.

one **girl**   two **girls**

b.

one **book** three _____

c.

one **stool** four _____

d.

one **hen**   five _____

e.

one **tree** three _____

f.

one **paper** two _____

g.

one **flower** several _____

h.

one **cat**   many _____

Introduction and Answers to Compound Words

National Literacy Strategy objectives

It is suggested that an understanding of compound words will help children break down longer words into their component parts:

Y2T2 W4: to split familiar oral and written compound words into their component parts, e.g. himself, handbag, milkman, pancake, teaspoon.

Note that the definition of a compound word (or 'word sum') is that both parts should be complete words with their own meanings.

Answers to page 74

1 starfish, grandfather, football, bathroom, blackbird, butterfly

2 goldfish, eyebrow, grasshopper, blacksmith

Answers to page 75

1 bulldog, blindfold, snowflake, farmyard, bedtime, eggcup

2 armchair, matchbox, eggshell, campfire

Compound Words

Name _____

1. **Complete each compound word.**

    Use these words.

father	ball	bird	room	fly	fish

    a. star_____

    b. grand_____

    c. foot_____

    d. bath_____

    e. black_____

    f. butter_____

2. **Choose the compound word that matches the picture.**

grasshopper	goldfish
eyebrow	blacksmith

    a. _____   b. _____

    c. _____   d. _____

Compound Words

Name _____

1. **Use a compound word to complete each sentence.**

> bedtime   snowflake   bulldog
> blindfold   eggcup   farmyard

a. The _____ bit the boy on the leg.

b. I put a _____ on so I couldn't see.

c. The hot sun melted the _____ .

d. We saw cows and pigs in the _____ .

e. As it is nine o'clock it is now my _____ .

f. I cracked the egg that was in the _____ .

2. **Match the pieces to make a compound word.**
Write the word on the line.

a.

arm ⟩ ⟨ noon
     ⟩ ⟨ chair

_____

b.

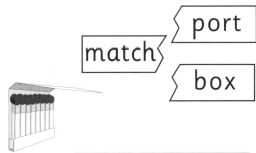

match ⟩ ⟨ port
      ⟩ ⟨ box

_____

c.

egg ⟩ ⟨ shell
    ⟩ ⟨ stick

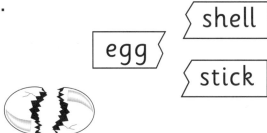

_____

d.

camp ⟩ ⟨ fire
     ⟩ ⟨ storm

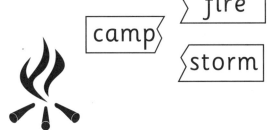

_____

Introduction to Revision Pages

This revision section provides worksheets that combine different spelling rules on one page, so that they offer general revision practice, for class use or for homework.

The main topics covered from the previous sections are:

- consonant clusters, at beginning and end of words

- double consonants, at the end and middle of words

- onset and rime

- vowel phonemes, especially long vowel phonemes

- word shapes, using visual memory techniques

- anagrams, as puzzle practice.

Revision Page

Name _____

Tips for improving your spelling:

1. Keep a list of words you spell incorrectly. Keep a notebook to write them in.

2. Learn to say words correctly. Say each syllable slowly, keeping a picture of the word in your mind.

3. Develop the dictionary habit. If you don't know how to spell a word, look it up in the dictionary. Try not to take the easy way out by always asking your parents or your teachers.

4. Become familiar with useful spelling rules and use them.

5. If you have guessed the spelling of a word, always check later to see if it is correct. Underline these words so you won't forget to check them when you have finished writing.

6. Remember to use the 'Look, cover, write, check' method.

Revision Page

Name _____

1. Add two letters to complete each word.

a. __c__ __l__ ock   b. __ __ um   c. __ __ uck

d. __ __ og   e. __ __ ag   f. __ __ oke

2. Complete each sentence.

Use these words.

gate   five   cake   tune   ride

a. I can eat a __**cake**__ .

b. I can open a _____ .

c. I can _____ a horse.

d. I can whistle a _____ .

e. The number after four is _____ .

Revision Page

Name _____

1. **Complete each word.**

   a. (gg ll)

   e_____

   b. (pp tt)

   pu_____y

   c. (dd ll)

   mi_____le

   d. (pp dd)

   ha_____y

2. **Unjumble each word.**

   a. wpa _____

   b. awter _____

   c. pnyo _____

   d. rcab _____

3. **Which words rhyme? Write them together.**

   | black | just | find | turn |

   a. rust _____

   b. mind _____

   c. burn _____

   d. track _____

Revision Page

Name _____

1. **Write each word in the correct pattern.**

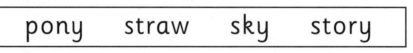

pony   straw   sky   story

a.

b.

c.

d.

2. **Complete each word.**

Use these.

oa   ea   ow   ay

a. f_____l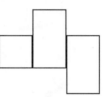

b. scr_____m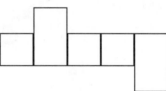

c. l____f

d. tr_____

3. **Write the correct word to match the picture.**

a. (pram tram)

_____

b. (flog flag)

_____

c. (frog frock)

_____

d. (stick stack)

_____

Revision Page

Name _____

1. Circle the correct word.

a. Michael wore his new (**boots** **roots**) to school.

b. Mice like to eat (**cheese** **sheep**).

c. The canary was in the (**cake** **cage**).

d. I tied a piece of (**coke** **rope**) around the parcel.

2. Circle the correct word.

a.

(brik   brick)

b.

(brush   brish)

c.

(wheat   wheet)

d.

(rabit   rabbit)

3. Complete each word.

a. (ou   or)

m_____se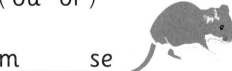

b. (ow   aw)

cr_____

c. (ou   aw)

cl_____d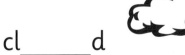

d. (ea   ew)

p_____ch

Revision Page

Name _____

1. **Add ir or ow to each word.**

    a. t___ ___n

    b. b___ ___d

    c. c___ ___cle

    d. cl___ ___n

2. **Complete each word.**

    Use these letters.

bb	tt	pp

    a. le___ ___er

    b. a___ ___le

    c. ra___ ___it

    d. ki___ ___en

3. **Find words in the grid. Write each one next to the word that rhymes.**

c	o	a	t	b
w	n	s	t	o
o	e	t	a	n
r	a	e	k	e
e	t	w	e	x

    a. tore _____

    b. boat _____

    c. grew _____

    d. seat _____

    e. cone _____

    f. rake _____

Revision Page

Name _____

1. **Add ai or or to complete each word.**

   a. tr___ ___n    b. h___ ___se

   c. f___ ___k   d. ch___ ___n

2. **What does it mean?**

   | yellow   winter   twenty   blind |

   Which word means –

   a. a colour? _____

   b. a cold season? _____

   c. unable to see? _____

   d. a number? _____

3. **Join the pieces and write the word.**

   a. (ch) + (urch) = _____

   b. (f) + (airy) = _____

   c. (fl) + (ower) = _____

   d. (b) + (owl) = _____

Revision Page

Name _____

1. **Complete each word.**

   Use these letters.

s	n	t	k	m	p

   a. ___ite

   b. ___ice

   c. ___ipe

   d. ___mile

   e. ___ine ⑨

   f. ___ime

2. **Complete each sentence using one of these words.**

bone	smoke	rope	hole

   a. The mouse ran through a _____ in the wall.

   b. A dog likes to chew a _____ .

   c. There was _____ coming from the fire.

   d. We tied the prisoner up with some _____ .

3. **Look at each word. Can you spot a smaller word in each one?**

   a. mine   **in**

   b. page   _____

   c. stop   _____

   d. land   _____

   e. rice   _____

   f. bite   _____

Revision Page

Name _____

1. **Add *oo* or *ee* to complete each word.**

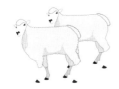

a. sh___ ___p   **b.** b___ ___k   **c.** m___ ___n

d. b___ ___t   **e.** s___ ___d   **f.** sp___ ___n

2. **Complete each sentence.**

Use these words.

cage   page   spade   late

a. We must hurry or we will be _____.

b. The bird was kept in a _____.

c. I dug the hole with a _____.

d. There are lots of pictures on this _____ of my book.

3. **Circle the correct word.**

a. wheel

cheese

weed

b. stool

noon

root

c. wave

rave   save

Revision Page

Name _____

1. **Circle the correct word.**

   a. A snail is a (pest   best) in the garden.

   b. I caught a (fish   wish) in the river.

   c. Bees live in a (hive   dive).

   d. If you heat water it will (soil   boil).

2. **Circle the word that matches the picture.**

   a. corn
      horn
      born

   b. cone
      zone
      bone

   c. hive
      dive
      five

   d. keep
      sheep
      weep

   e. lice
      rice
      mice

   f. card
      carp
      cart

3. **Look at the words in the box. Write the word pairs together.**

   | seat   bead   bash   heat |
   | cake   cash   bake   read |

   a. __**seat**__ __**heat**__   b. _____ _____

   c. _____ _____   d. _____ _____

Revision Page

Name _____

1. **Join the pieces and write the word.**

    a. (wh) + (eat)

    = _____

    b. (wh) + (ale)

    = _____

    c. (tr) + (uck)

    = _____

    d. (fr) + (ock)

    = _____

2. **Add _ea_ or _oa_ to complete each word.**

    a. g___ ___t

    b. m___ ___t

    c. c___ ___t

    d. s___ ___t

3. **What does it mean?**

snail   pine   horse   jaw

    Which word means –

    a. a type of tree? _____

    b. a large animal we ride? _____

    c. part of your face? _____

    d. an animal with a shell? _____

87

Revision Page

Name _____

1. **Circle the word that does not contain the same letter pattern.**

   a. hat   chat   that   nice

   b. rest   sell   pest   best

   c. boot   feet   sheet   meet

   d. queer   four   steer   beer

2. **Complete each sentence.**

   Use these words.

whale   pale   sale   tale

   a. We bought the bike at a _____.

   b. Our teacher told us a _____ about snakes.

   c. We saw a large _____ in the ocean.

   d. The colour of his skin is quite _____.

3. **Find all the words in the grid.**

b	a	l	l	f
w	a	l	l	a
h	a	l	l	l
t	a	l	l	l

   a. Be careful you don't _____ off the roof.

   b. I can bounce a _____.

   c. Humpty Dumpty sat on a _____.

   d. Mike is short but Asha is _____.

   e. The dance was held in a large _____.

Revision Page

Name _____

1. **Find words ending in *ew*. Use each word in the correct sentence.**

   | flew   sew   crew   drew |

   a. Ali _____ a picture.

   b. John began to _____ the cloth.

   c. The bird _____ to its nest.

   d. The _____ boarded the ship.

2. **Draw a line from the word to the picture.**

   a. mill
   hill
   fill

   b. hide
   tide
   bride

   c. boat
   coat
   goat

3. **Complete each word.**

   Use these letters.

   | oot   old   ite   ell |

   a. b_____

   b. g_____

   c. sh_____

   d. k_____

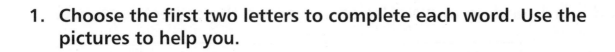
Revision Page

Name _____

1. **Choose the first two letters to complete each word. Use the pictures to help you.**

    a. (bl cr)

    _____y

    b. (dr cr)

    _____ip

    c. (fl cl)

    _____ag

    d. (sk st)

    _____ool

2. **Make three words that start with the same letters.**

    Use these letters.

sk	fr	st	tr

    a. **sk** in   **b.** _____og   **c.** _____ep   **d.** _____ee

    sk y   _____ock   _____ar   _____y

    sk ip   _____ee   _____op   _____ip

3. **Look at the pictures. Complete each word.**

    a. _____oom    **b.** _____ow

Revision Page

1. **Group these words. The first one has been done for you.**

mail	snail	sack	fall
harm	~~back~~	farm	ball

    a. ack   b. ail   c. all   d. arm

    back   _____   _____   _____

    _____   _____   _____   _____

2. **Which word is out of place? Draw a circle around it.**

a.	b.	c.	d.
hear	seed	from	lice
near	boot	send	ice
dear	weed	lend	mice
(ball)	feed	mend	book

e.	f.	g.	h.
fish	side	hood	hook
dish	tide	wood	chair
sing	ride	clock	took
wish	table	food	book

3. **Complete each word family.**

    Use these words.

dive	~~gone~~	cash	late

a.	b.	c.	d.
cone	bash	mate	give
bone	wash	date	live
done	splash	plate	five

    gone   _____   _____   _____

91

Revision Page

Name _____

Rearrange the letters to make a word that fits the picture.
The first one has been done for you.

a. rnai

| rain |

b. stne

| |

c. hpsi

| |

d. mrdu

| |

e. tgae

| |

f. kcae

| |

g. odor

| |

h. tars

| |

i. lebl

| |

j. urfo

| |

k. rpoe

| |

l. hira

| |

Revision Page

Name _____

Rearrange the letters to make a word that fits the picture.

a. low   **owl**

b. god   _____

c. nip   _____

d. ram   _____

e. sub   _____

f. act   _____

g. tar   _____

h. was   _____

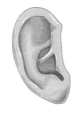

i. are   _____

j. but   _____

k. net   _____

l. pat   _____

m. ape   _____

n. eat   _____

o. ten   _____

Answers to Revision Pages

Answers to page 78

1 drum, truck, frog, flag, smoke

2 gate, ride, tune, five

Answers to page 79

1 egg, puppy, middle, happy

2 paw, water, pony, crab

3
rust, just;
mind, find;
burn, turn;
track, black

Answers to page 80

1 straw, sky, pony, story

2 fowl, scream, loaf, tray

3 pram, flag, frock, stick

Answers to page 81

1 boots, cheese, cage, rope

2 brick, brush, wheat, rabbit

3 mouse, crow, cloud, peach

Answers to page 82

1 town, bird, circle, clown

2 letter, apple, rabbit, kitten

3 wore, coat, stew, neat, bone, take

Answers to page 83

1 train, horse, fork, chain

2 yellow, winter, blind, twenty

3 church, fairy, flower, bowl

Answers to page 84

1 kite, mice, pipe, smile, nine, time

2 hole, bone, smoke, rope

3 in, age, top, and, ice, bit

Answers to page 85

1 sheep, book, moon, boot, seed, spoon

2 late, cage, spade, page

3 cheese, stool, wave

Answers to Revision Pages

Answers to page 86

1 pest, fish, hive, boil

2 horn, cone, dive, weep, rice, carp

3
bead, read;
bash, cash;
cake, bake

Answers to page 87

1 wheat, whale, truck, frock

2 goat, meat, coat, seat

3 pine, horse, jaw, snail

Answers to page 88

1 nice, sell, boot, four

2 sale, tale, whale, pale

3 fall, ball, wall, tall, hall

Answers to page 89

1 drew, sew, flew, crew

2 hill, bride, boat

3 boot, gold, shell, kite

Answers to page 90

1 cry, drip, flag, stool

2
frog, frock, free;
step, star, stop;
tree, try, trip;

3 broom, crow

Answers to page 91

1
back, sack;
mail, snail;
fall, ball;
harm, farm

2 boot, from, book, sing, table, clock, chair

3 cash, late, dive

Answers to page 92

rain, nest, ship, drum, gate, cake, door, star, bell, four, rope, hair

Answers to page 93

dog, pin, arm, bus, cat, rat, saw, ear, tub, ten, tap, pea, tea, net

My own spelling lists

Name _____

_____   _____

_____   _____

_____   _____

_____   _____

_____   _____

_____   _____

_____   _____

_____   _____

_____   _____

_____   _____

_____   _____

_____   _____

_____   _____